THE WHITE HOUSE

AMERICAN SYMBOLS

Lynda Sorensen

The Rourke Book Company, Inc.
Vero Beach, Florida 32964

PHOTO CREDITS
Courtesy Washington, D.C., Visitors and Convention Bureau: cover;
courtesy National Park Service: title page (William Clark), page 18
(William Clark); © Frank Balthis: page 4; © The White House
Historical Association: pages 7, 8, 10, 15, 17, 21; courtesy National
Archives: pages 12-13

Library of Congress Cataloging-in-Publication Data

Sorensen, Lynda, 1953–
    The White House / by Lynda Sorensen
        p. cm. — (American symbols)
    Includes index.
    ISBN 1-55916-050-0
        1. White House (Washington, D.C.)—Juvenile literature.
2. Washington (D.C.)—Buildings, structures, etc.—Juvenile
literature. 3. Presidents—United States—Juvenile literature.
[1. White House (Washington, D.C.) 2. Presidents.]
I. Title II. Series.
F204.W5S68 1994
975.3—dc20   94–7055
                                                     CIP
Printed in the USA   AC

TABLE OF CONTENTS

The White House   5
A Symbol of Freedom   6
Building The White House   9
Public Rooms   11
The East Room   14
Private Rooms   16
The White House Grounds   19
Changes in the White House   20
The White House Burns   22
Glossary   23
Index   24

THE WHITE HOUSE

The White House is where the President of the United States lives and works. The White House is in Washington, D.C., which is the **capital** city of the United States. George Washington, the first president, chose the place where the White House was built.

The White House used to be called the President's House, the President's Palace and the Executive **Mansion**. President Theodore Roosevelt changed the name to White House in 1902.

Chrysanthemums bloom in a garden across the street from the White House in Washington, D.C.

A SYMBOL OF FREEDOM

The White House helps **symbolize**, or stand for, American freedom and democracy. Democracy is a government in which people are free to elect their leaders.

The president who lives in the White House is chosen by America's voters.

An American president does not own the White House. A president lives there only during his time in office. Voters freely elect a president every four years.

George Washington was the first president of the United States

BUILDING THE FIRST WHITE HOUSE

WASHINGTON D.C. 1798

BUILDING THE WHITE HOUSE

The United States government held a contest in 1792. People were invited to enter drawings of a house for the president. **Architect** James Hoban's design of a three-story mansion was chosen.

The new home was not finished in time for George Washington. But in 1800, the country's second president, John Adams, moved into the partly finished home. George Washington was the only president who never lived in the White House.

"Building the First White House," a painting by N.C. Wyeth, shows George Washington (left) looking at the new president's mansion

PUBLIC ROOMS

Visitors are allowed in just a small part of the 132-room White House. Some of the rooms open to the public are the East Room, the State Dining Room, the Red Room, the Blue Room and the Green Room.

During a tour, visitors can see furniture and other objects used by past presidents.

The White House Red Room is sometimes open during tours of the White House

A crowd gathers on the White House lawn in 1903 for the annual Easter egg roll

THE EAST ROOM

The white and gold East Room is the largest room in the White House. Guests of the president often gather here before an important dinner meeting. Singers, dancers and musicians perform in the East Room.

Daughters of presidents have been married in the East Room. The funerals of five presidents were held there.

President Theodore Roosevelt's children found the huge East Room perfect for roller skating!

The East Room is the largest room in the White House

PRIVATE ROOMS

Most of the White House rooms are private. The living quarters for the president and the president's family are on the second floor. The third floor has rooms for the president's many guests.

Other private rooms include a library, bowling alley, swimming pool, movie theater and the president's Oval Office.

Former President Bush working in the Oval Office of the White House

THE WHITE HOUSE GROUNDS

The White House is surrounded by 18 acres of lawn and gardens. Except on a few special days, the lawn and gardens are not open to visitors.

On the Monday following Easter the lawn area opens to children for an egg-rolling contest. The gardens open for a public tour in springtime.

Tulips bloom in a White House garden

CHANGES IN THE WHITE HOUSE

The White House was almost 150 years old in 1948, and it was beginning to fall apart. President Harry Truman and his family moved out of the White House so that it could be rebuilt.

Nearly every part of the White House, except the outer stone walls, was rebuilt. After four years, the Trumans moved back into a brand new White House.

In 1948 construction workers began to rebuild the White House

THE WHITE HOUSE BURNS

During America's War of 1812 with Great Britain, British soldiers marched into Washington, D. C. President James Madison and his wife, Dolly, were whisked away.

British soldiers burned the White House to the ground. Only stone walls remained. Dolly Madison rescued a portrait of George Washington before she left the White House. Workmen began to rebuild the White House in 1817.

Glossary

architect (ARK uh tekt) — someone who designs buildings, gardens and certain other things

capital (KAP uh tul) — the city in which a state, province or nation has its center of government

mansion (MAN shun) — a large and expensive home

symbolize (SIM bull ize) — to stand for, or represent, something, as a flag symbolizes a certain country

INDEX

Blue Room   11
capital   5
democracy   6
East Room   11, 14
Executive Mansion   5
funerals   14
gardens   19
government   6
Great Britain   22

Green Room   11
mansion   9
Oval Office   16
presidents   5, 6, 11, 14, 16
Red Room   11
State Dining Room   11
voters   6
War of 1812   20
Washington, D.C.   5